FRACTIONS FLIP BOOKS

illustrated by
Dwayne Douglas Kohn

Smart As A Fox Teaching Materials are available from your local teacher supply store or purchase online at: www.MisterKindergarten.com. For materials in Spanish, please visit: www.PrimerGrado.com. We publish over 400 titles in a variety of languages.

SMART AS A FOX
OCEANSIDE, CALIFORNIA

FRACTIONS FLIP BOOKS

So easy to create and so simple to use! You and your students will LOVE making and using these fun Flip Books! Now your students can play with their food!

Simply color the drawings, cut out the "pages" and staple them where indicated. The predictable format guarantees that your students will experience success with fractions right away using real world examples!

Before making the booklets, introduce your students to the concept of fractions. Draw a large circle on the board and tell the students that it is a pizza. Draw a line down the middle of the "pizza," cutting it into two equal pieces. Explain that there are now two slices of pizza. If you eat one of the two slices, you have eaten half of the pizza, which is 1 out of 2, or 1/2.

Now divide the pizza again so that there are four equal pieces. Show them that now if you eat one slice of the pizza it is only 1/4 of the pizza; or one out of 4 slices. However, if you eat two of the four slices, you have eaten 2/4 of the pizza. Ask them if they think that 2/4 is the same as 1/2. Some students might not see the two fractions as being the same and will need to see both examples side by side for comparison.

Our hamburger flip booklet is a very simple one that reviews the concept of half. This is a good booklet to make to reinforce the concept of half after demonstrating with the pizza drawing the idea of fractions.

The ice cream cone, with three scoops of ice cream, introduces the idea of thirds. Be sure to staple the scoops on top so that students can flip them up to review 1/3, 2/3 and 3/3.

We have include two booklets to work on fourths; a glass of juice (or milk) and a tasty sandwich. Staple the "pages" where indicated to make these two flip books. The liquid in the glass "disappears" as the pages are turned, revealing new fractions each time.

Staple the "sandwich" to the paper plate and then "slice" the sandwich into four equal pieces by folding back one section at a time to create 4/4, 3/4, 2/4 and 1/4. Emphasize that whenever the denominator and the numerator are the same, such as 4/4, it really means one whole.

Your students will love "slicing" the pizza to make *sixths*, "cutting" the cake to discover *eighths*, and "eating" the chocolate bar to see *ninths*.

Our final booklet introduces *tenths* by having the students count the apples to see how many of them are red.

Once finished, these flip booklets can be sent home so that these new fraction skills can be reviewed with the family.

Learning fractions has never been so much fun.... or so tasty. Bon Appétit!

Hungry for Half of a Hamburger?

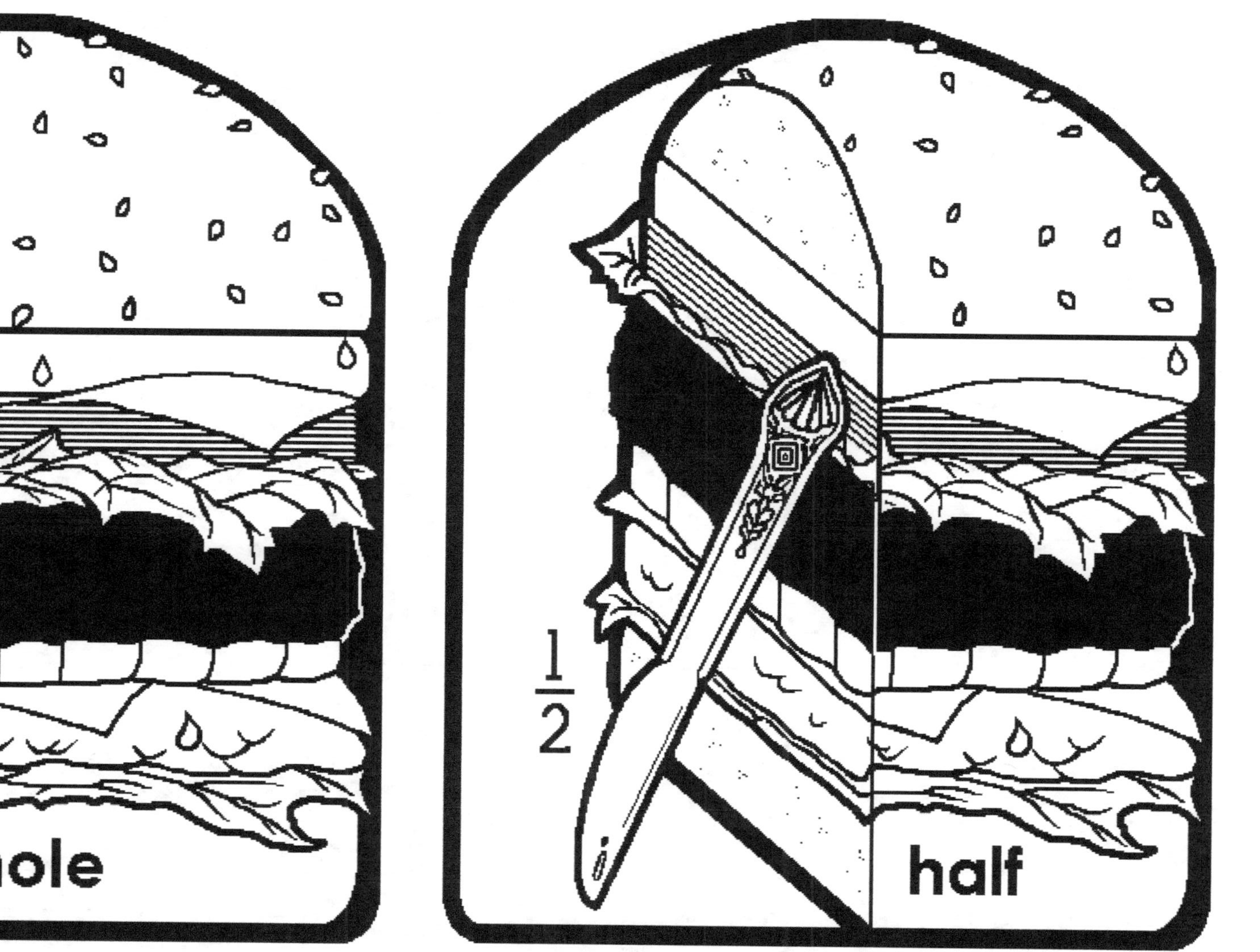

Staple pages together to make a mini-booklet.

www.MisterKindergarten.com

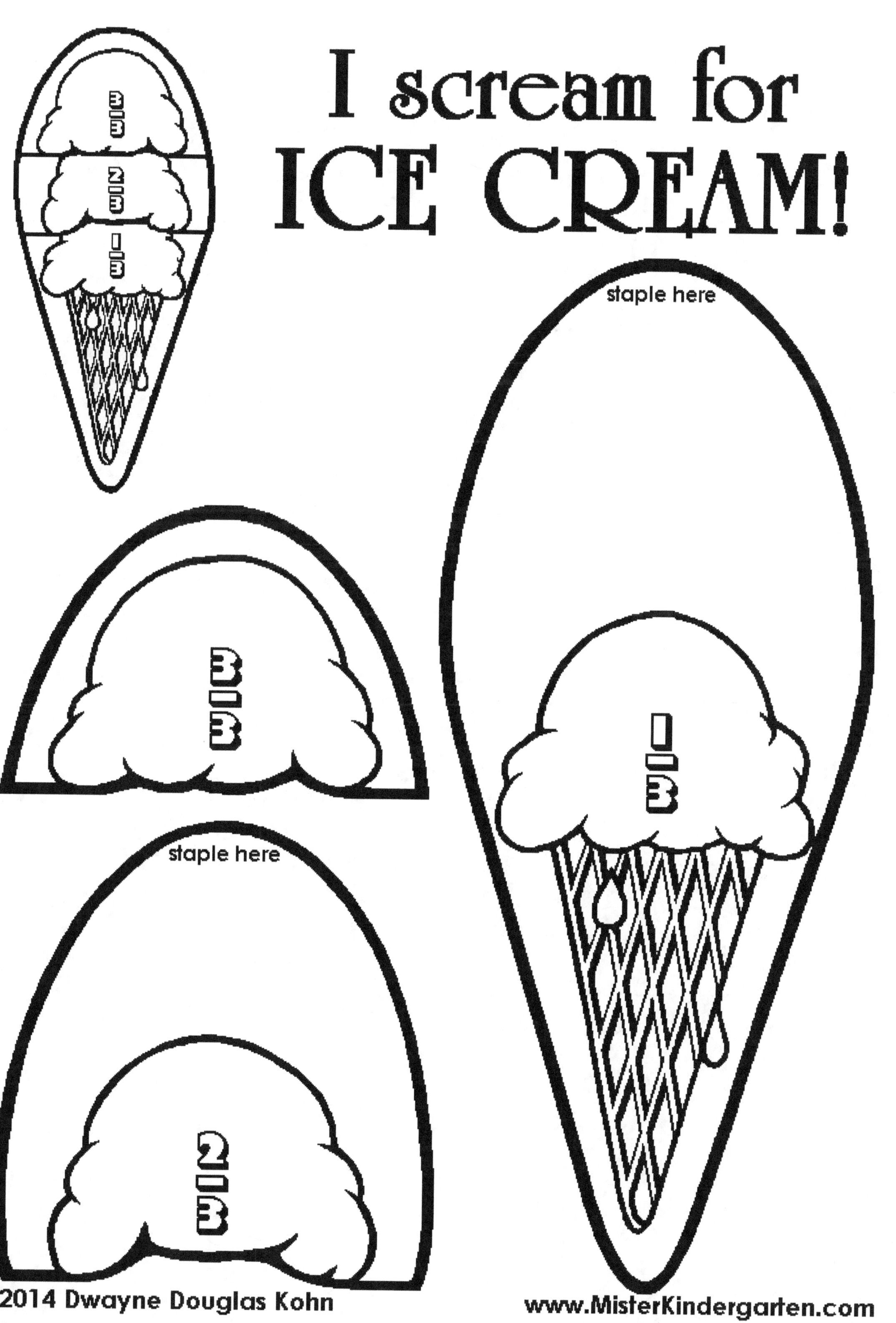
I scream for
ICE CREAM!
staple here
staple here
3/3
2/3
1/3
3/3
2/3
1/3
©2014 Dwayne Douglas Kohn
www.MisterKindergarten.com

THIRSTY FOR FRACTIONS!

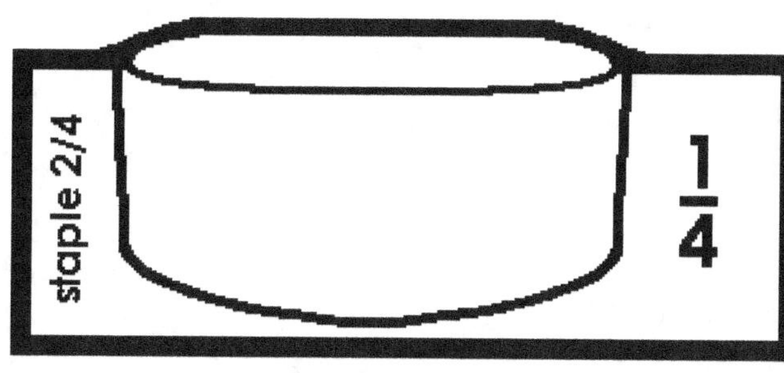

INSTRUCTIONS:
Color the pieces. Cut out pieces. Staple together as indicated. Open flaps to see the drink disappear into new fractions!

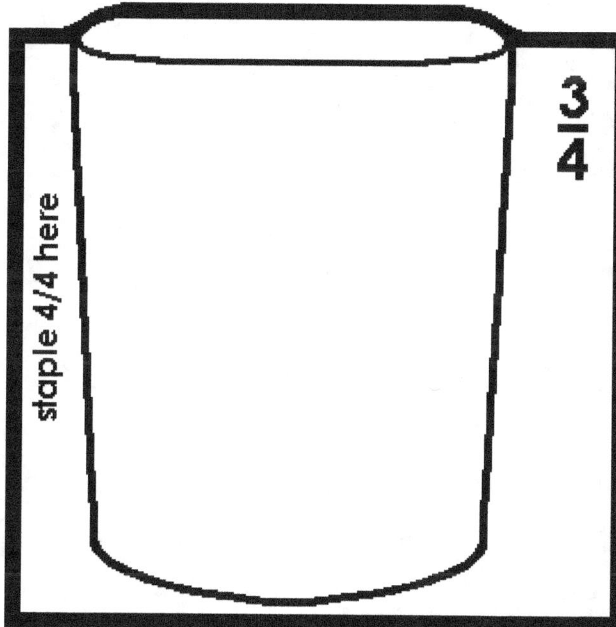

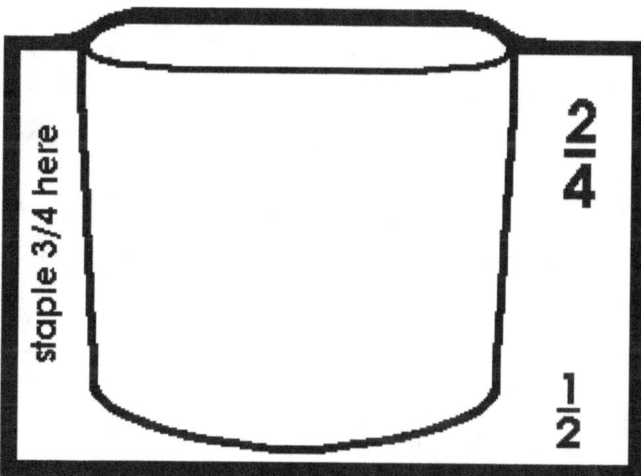

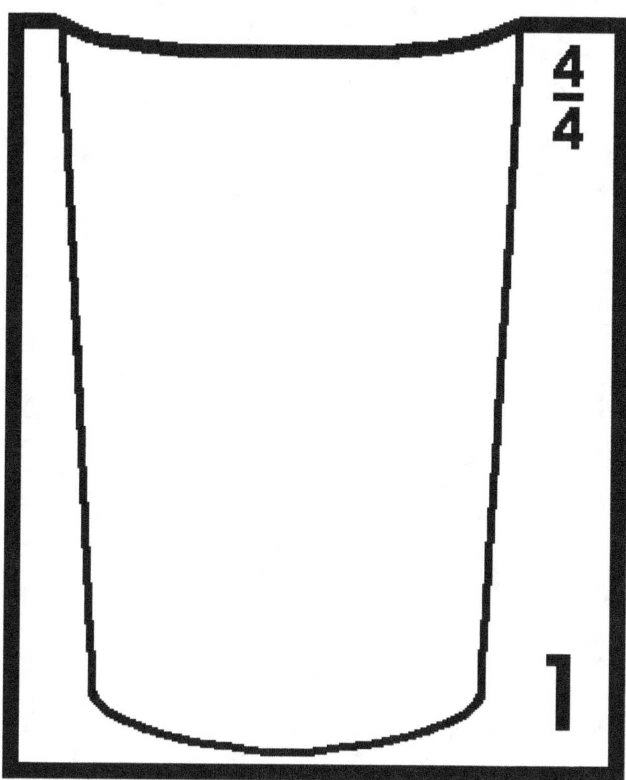

©2014 Dwayne Douglas Kohn

www.MisterKindergarten.com

Can you eat a whole sandwich?

1. Color and carefully cut out the four pieces of the sandwich.
2. Color and carefully cut out the plate (next page).
3. Staple piece " A" first where indicated on the plate.
4. Staple the other three pieces where indicated on the plate.
5. "Eat" 1/4 of the sandwich by folding back one piece.

Can you make 3/4, 2/4 (1/2) and 1/4 of a sandwich?

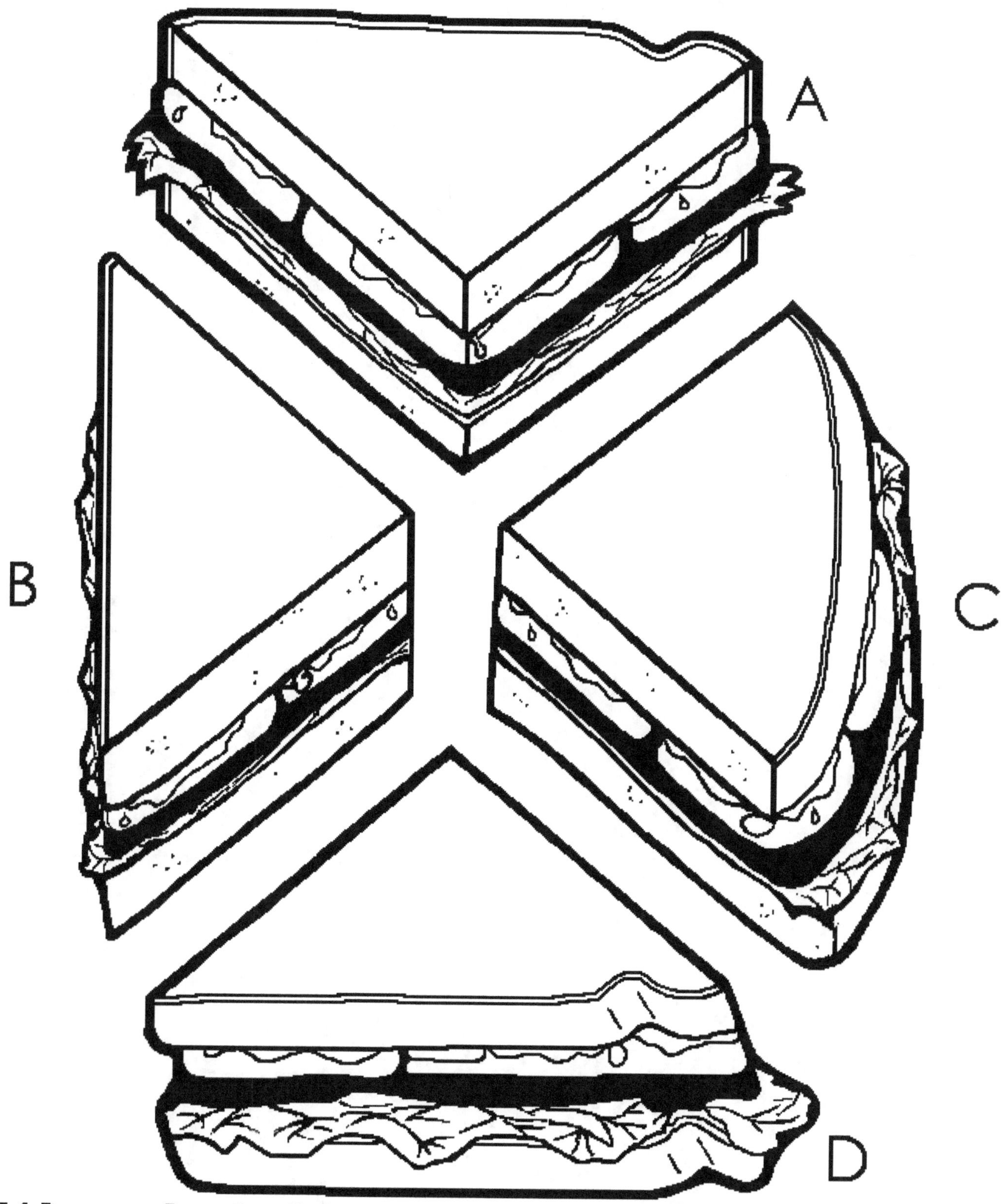

     www.MisterKindergarten.com

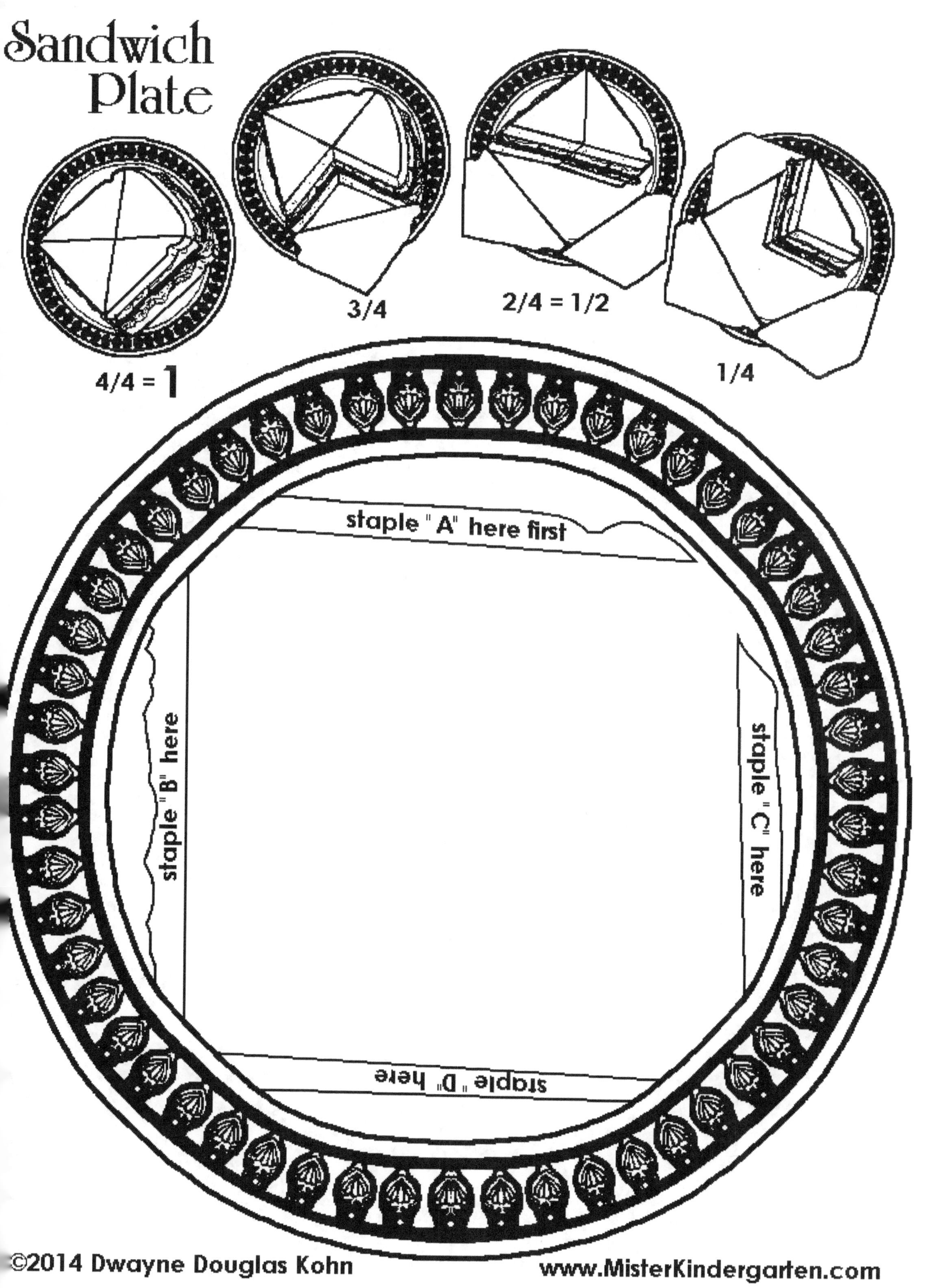

Sandwich Plate
4/4 = 1
3/4
2/4 = 1/2
1/4
staple " A " here first
staple " B " here
staple " C " here
staple " D " here
©2014 Dwayne Douglas Kohn
www.MisterKindergarten.com

A Piece of Pizza

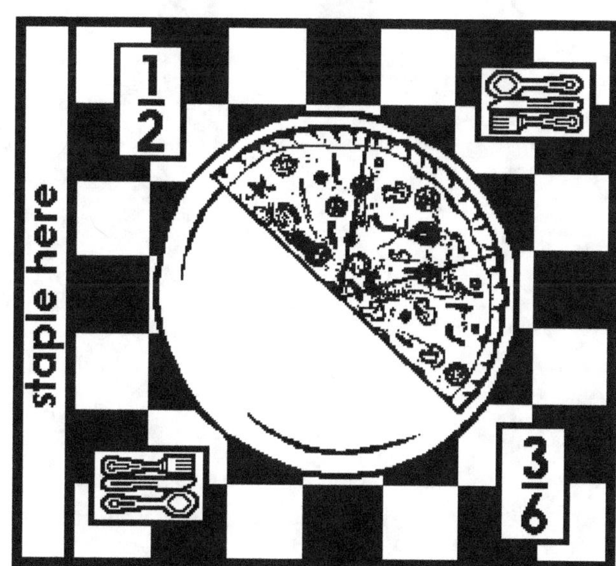

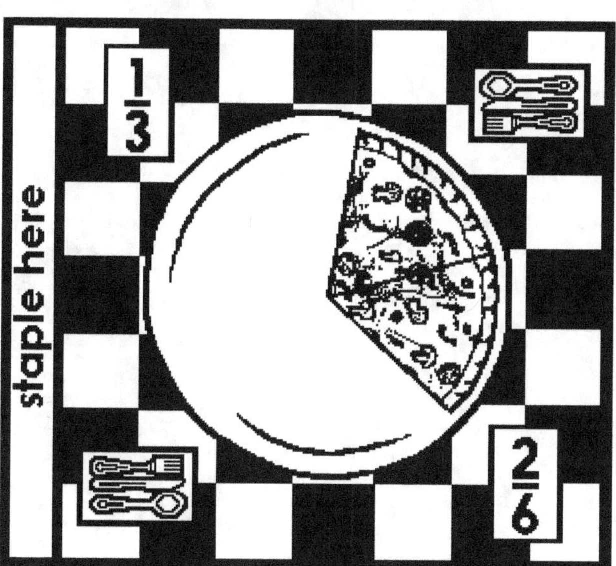

Cut the Cake!

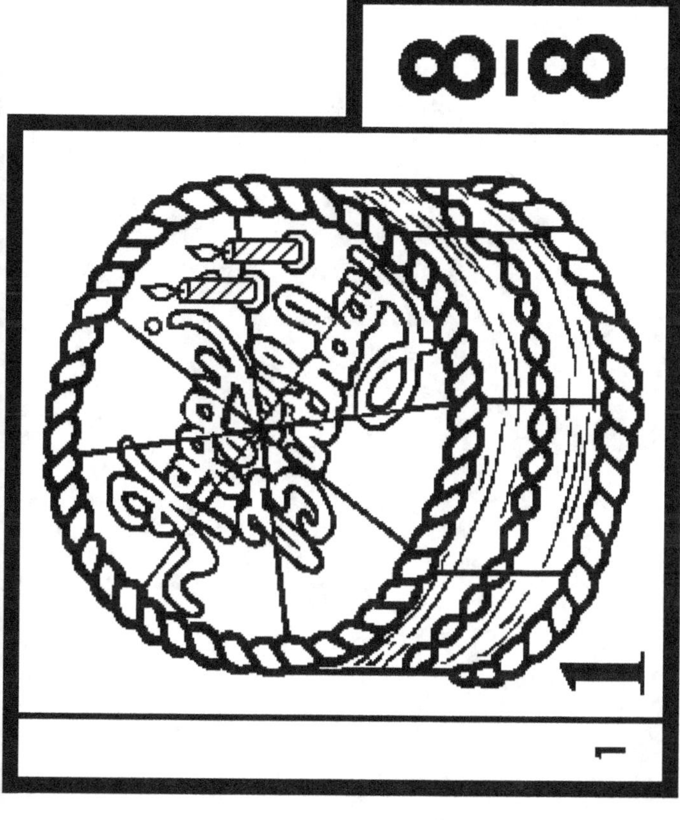

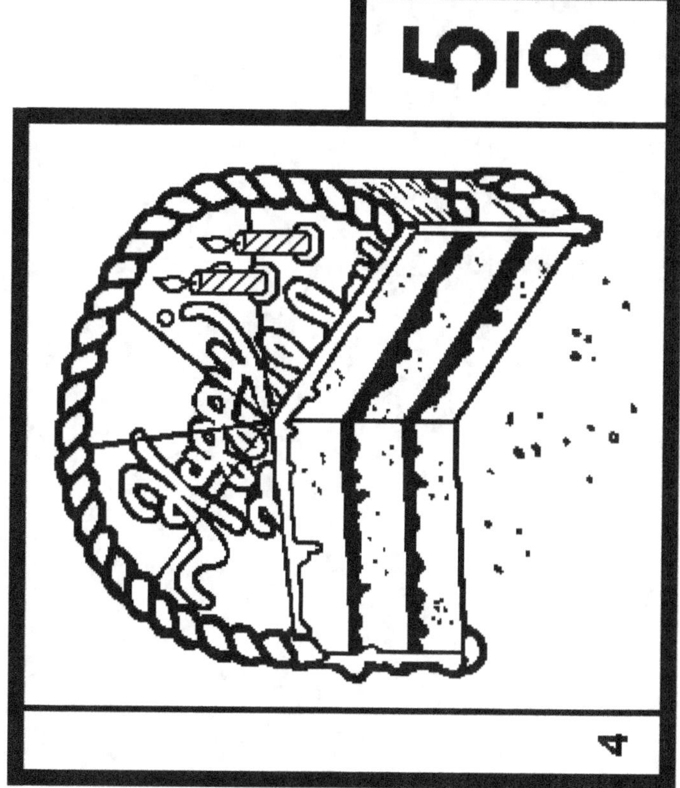

Cut the Cake!

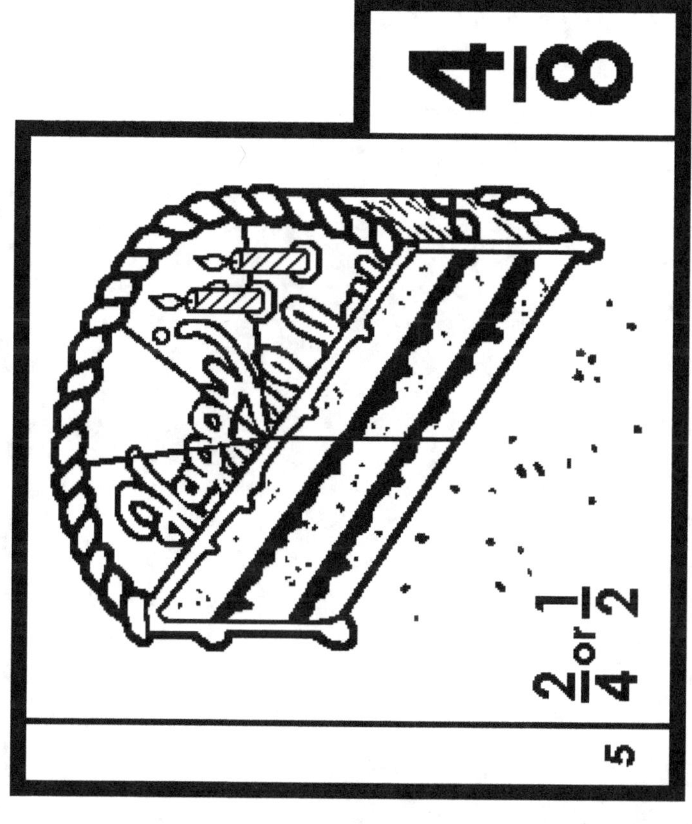

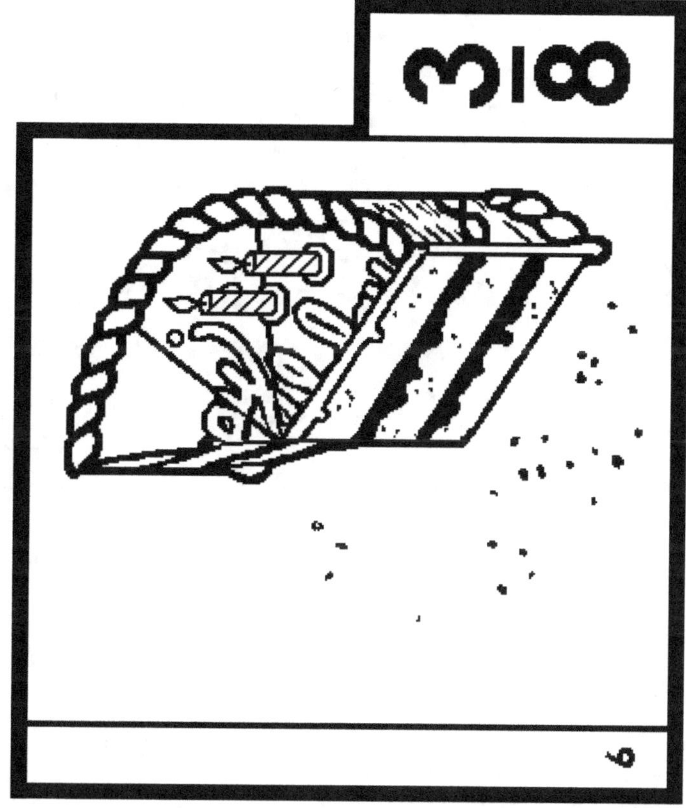

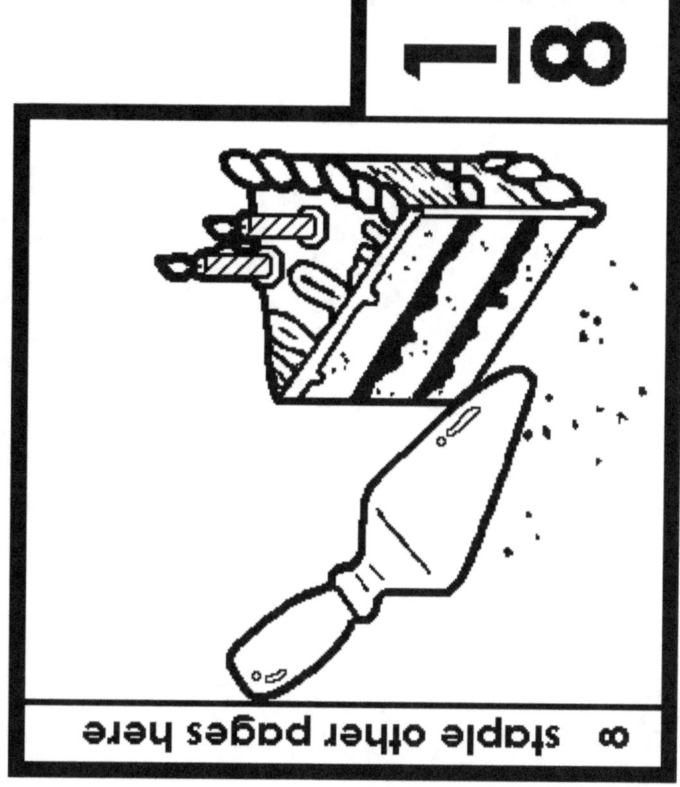

©2014 Dwayne Douglas Kohn   www.MisterKindergarten.com

WHO ATE ALL OF THE CHOCOLATE?

cover   **page 1**

CHOCOLATE BAR INSTRUCTIONS:
1. Carefully cut out the pages.
2. Put in order starting with 1/9 on the bottom.
3. Put the cover (wrapper) on top.
4. Staple the booklet together on the left side.

        www.MisterKindergarten.com

CHOCOLATE BAR PART 2

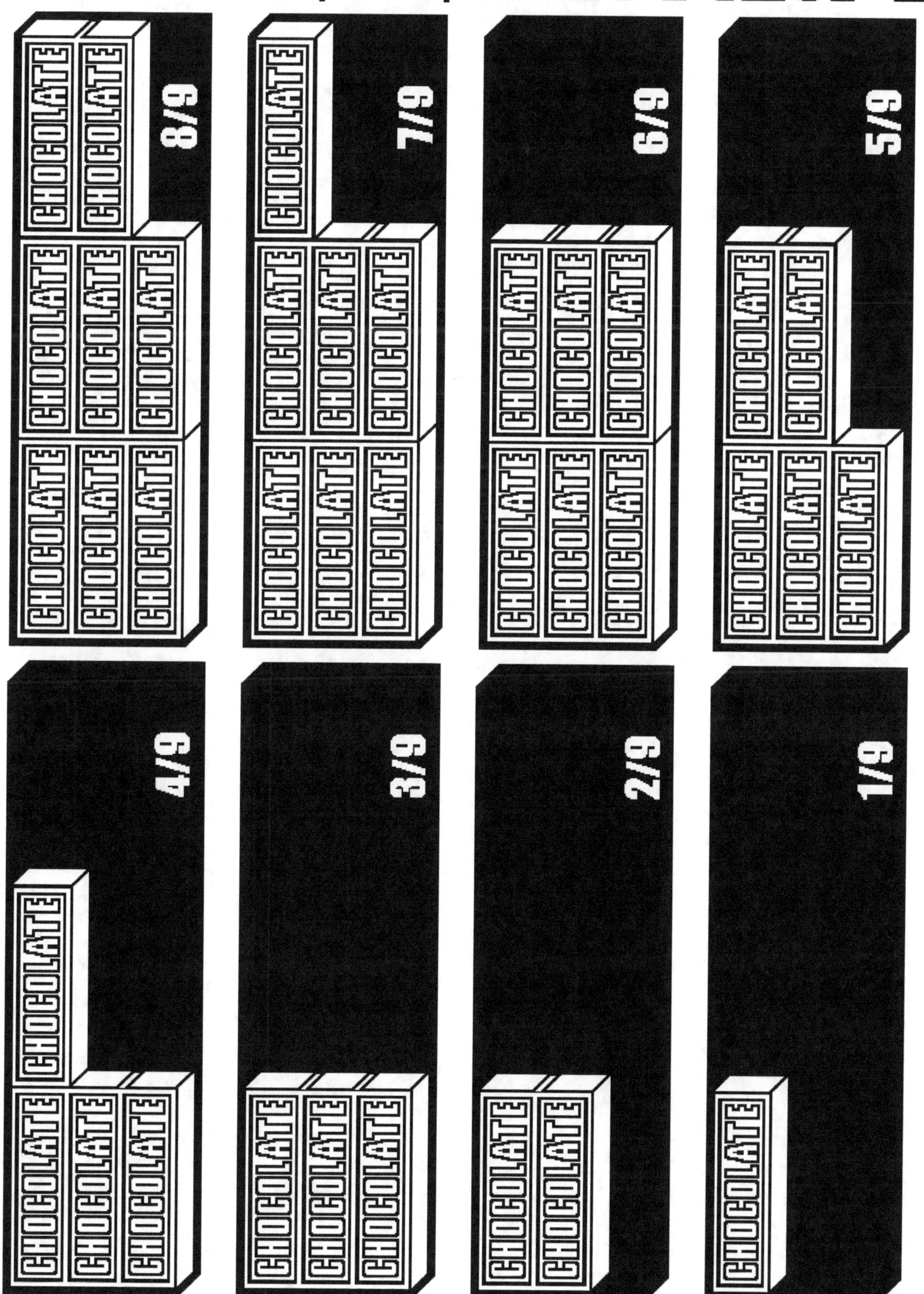

www.MisterKindergarten.com

©2014 Dwayne Douglas Kohn

www.MisterKindergarten.com

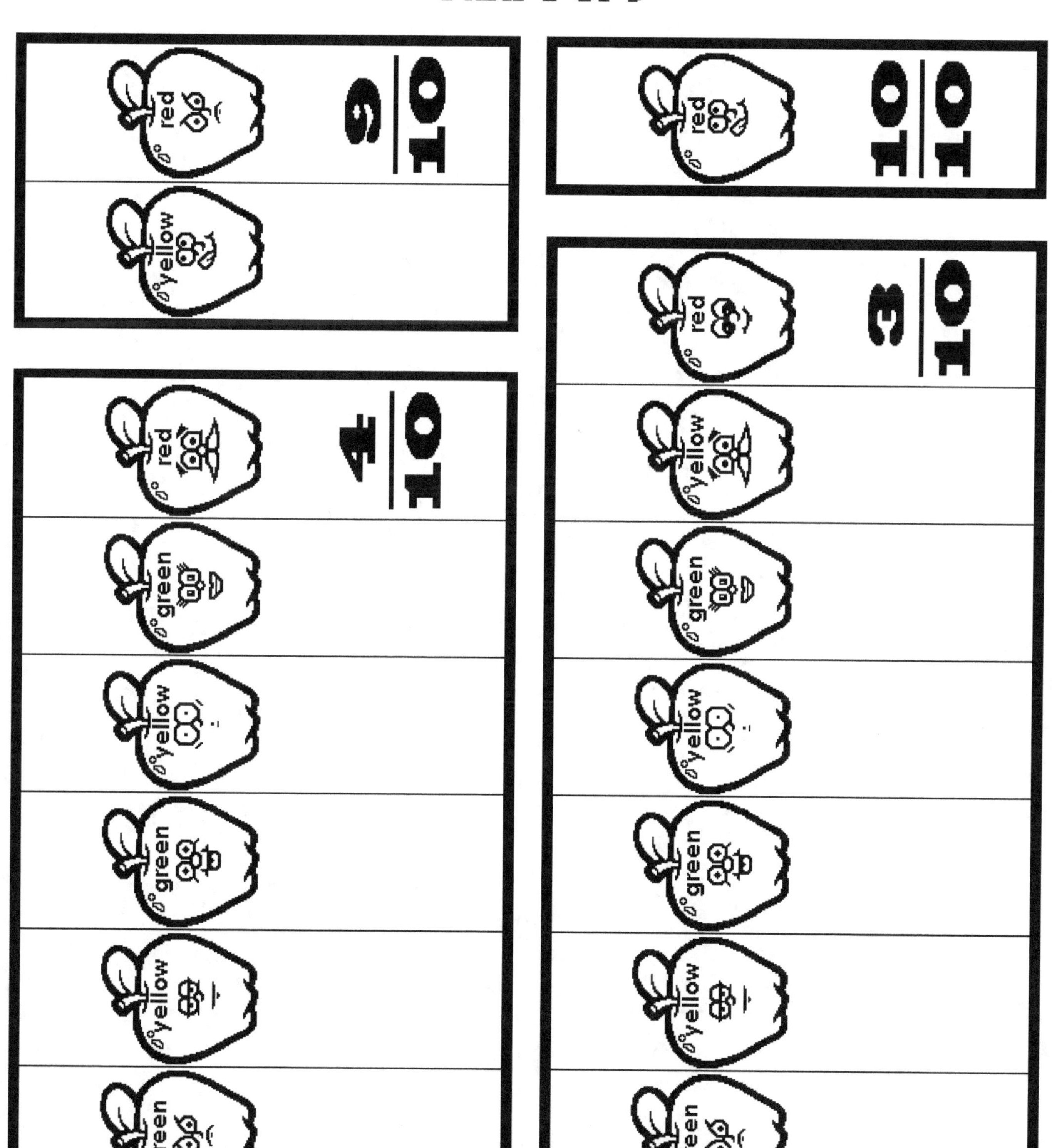

www.MisterKindergarten.com

www.MisterKindergarten.com

www.ingramcontent.com/pod-product-compliance
Lightning Source LLC
Chambersburg PA
CBHW080924160726

48000CB00009B/3122